FORTIFY

©Daniel Hagen 2023

First published Daniel Hagen Ministries

www.danielhagenministries.com

All rights reserved. Without limiting the rights under copyright reserved above, no part of this publication may be reproduced, stored in or introduced into a database and retrieval system or transmitted in any form or any means (electronic, mechanical, photocopying, recording or otherwise) without the prior written permission of both the owner of the copyright and the above publishers. The only exception is brief quotations in printed reviews.

Printed by IngramSpark
ISBN: 978-0-6454722-7-1
ISBN Ebook: 978-0-6454722-6-4

Unless otherwise specified, all scripture taken from the New King James Version®, Copyright© 1982 by Thomas Nelson. Used by permission. All rights reserved.

Cover design by Samantha Griffiths

CONTENTS

ACKNOWLEGEMENTS

INTRODUCTION

SESSION 1
The Nature of Faith

SESSION 2
Foundations of Faith

SESSION 3
Building a Strong Faith Foundation:
Understanding our Identity in Christ.

SESSION 4
Walking in our Identity in Christ

SESSION 5
Freedom and Deliverance:
Understanding Deliverance

SESSION 6
Maintaining Freedom after Deliverance

SESSION 7
God's Promise of Healing:
Walking in Divine Health

SESSION 8
Maintaining Healing and Divine Health

SESSION 9
Living a Victorious Life:
Understanding Victory in Christ

SESSION 10
Walking out a Victorious Life

SESSION 11
Personal Spiritual Development:
Developing a Personal Prayer Life

SESSION 12
Consistency and Growth in Faith

SESSION 13
Final Reflections:
Moving Forward in your Fortified Faith Journey

DECLARATIONS

ACKNOWLEDGEMENTS

I would like to thank Bev and Anton Bekker for your role in reviewing and editing this work book. Your ongoing support and encouragement is very much appreciated.

I'd like to thank Samantha Griffiths for the design on the cover art.

Finally I'd love to thank my amazing family including my wife Chelsea and children, Reece, Esther, Caleb and Abigail. I love you all very much

INTRODUCTION

God has an extraordinary way of guiding us, and the birth of this study book, **'Fortify,'** is a testament to that. It began with a prophetic dream I had in which the Lord vividly depicted a huge wave of revival hitting the world. It was a wave unlike any other - rich with deliverance from demonic strongholds, divine healing, and a bountiful harvest of souls being brought into the Kingdom.

My mandate from God was clear:
"Help my people get revival ready and help my people be fortified in their faith"

In response to this divine mandate, I was compelled to write this book.

'Fortify' is more than just a title - it's a spiritual directive for every believer. Our faith, just like any fortress, requires constant reinforcement to withstand the battles it encounters. The Lord desires His people to be fortified in their faith, resilient in the face of trials, and relentless in their pursuit of His Kingdom and His righteousness.
As we anticipate this great revival, we need to be firmly grounded in our faith. It's not enough to participate or merely spectate, we must learn to balance the awe-inspiring move of the Spirit in signs and wonders on the one hand, and a profound understanding of God's Word on the other.

In **'Fortify,'** we delve into the Scriptures to deepen our understanding of God's promises and our identity in Christ. It's a guide to:
obtaining and maintaining deliverance, embracing divine health, and embodying the victorious life that God has planned for each of us.

God does not want us to be in a place where we need ongoing deliverance and be stuck in a cycle. He wants us to get free and stay free. My prayer is that through the pages of this study book, you will be equipped to stand firm in your faith, keep the freedom that Christ has won for you, and walk out a victorious Christian life.

INTRODUCTION

My life was a mess before I walked into a local church and heard the message of salvation. That day, the power of the Gospel, the *dunamis* power of God, broke the chains of sin and set me free.

The moment I accepted Christ, I felt a shift in my spirit, a liberation from the darkness that had clouded my life. I was 'born again', a new creation in Christ, and the old things had passed away **(2 Corinthians 5:17)**.

My journey from darkness to light wasn't without challenges, but the grace of God was always there to see me through. I had to learn to submit to God and resist the devil **(James 4:7),** and with every step of obedience, I felt the demonic influences lose their grip over me.

I delved into the scriptures, fortifying my faith and renewing my mind with the truths of God's word.

The change wasn't just in the spiritual realm; it was visible to those around me. They saw a man transformed by the power of God. And it wasn't just about me; God had a bigger plan. He wanted to use my life, my testimony, to impact others. He led me to write the book 'Ignite the Dynamite', a detailed account of my journey from sin and demonic bondage to freedom and victory in Christ.

I'm living proof that God's grace is sufficient, His power made perfect in weakness **(2 Corinthians 12:9**). If He could save a 'wretch' like me, He can save anyone.

Today, I'm committed to helping others experience this life-transforming power of God, to help them fortify their faith and walk in the victory that is already theirs in Christ. God has a plan for each one of us, plans for good and not for evil, to give us a future and a hope **(Jeremiah 29:11)**. All we need to do is believe and receive it.

It's my prayer that this book, 'Fortify', will help you do just that.

This study book is a call to ready ourselves, to bolster our faith, to understand our divine authority, and to passionately engage in the revival that's before us.

THIS IS A CALL TO 'FORTIFY'!

THE NATURE OF FAITH

Defining Faith

Faith, as described in the Bible, is a confident assurance and trust in God and His promises; unseen yet deeply felt and manifested in our lives.

In the book of **Hebrews**, we are given a clear definition,

"Now faith is the assurance of things hoped for, the conviction of things not seen" **(Hebrews 11:1)**.

This element of trust in the unseen is vividly illustrated in the story of Abraham. Despite being very old and without a natural ability to bear children, Abraham trusted God's promise that he would become a "father of many nations" **(Genesis 17:4-5)**. This trust was not based on his physical capabilities, but purely on God's promise.

Another example can be seen in the New Testament with the Roman Centurion in **Matthew 8:5-13**. **The Centurion's servant** was paralysed, but he believed that if Jesus merely spoke a word, his servant would be healed. Jesus marvelled at this great faith, which relied not on physical evidence but on a firm conviction in His divine authority and power.

Both examples encapsulate the essence of faith - unwavering trust and assurance in God's promises, irrespective of the seen circumstances.

THE NATURE OF FAITH

Scriptural Basis for Faith

The scriptural basis for faith lies primarily in the truth and infallibility of God's Word. **Romans 10:17** says,

"So then faith comes by hearing, and hearing by the word of God."

This verse emphasises that our faith begins and grows through a consistent intake of God's Word, allowing us to internalise His promises and principles. As we immerse ourselves in the Word, we understand God's character and His unfailing love for us, which bolsters our faith in Him.

Another important scripture that speaks to how we get faith is **Mark 11:22-24**, where Jesus tells His disciples,

"Have faith in God. Truly, I say to you, whoever says to this mountain, 'Be taken up and thrown into the sea,' and does not doubt in his heart, but believes that what he says will come to pass, it will be done for him. Therefore I tell you, whatever you ask in prayer, believe that you have received it, and it will be yours."

Here, Jesus emphasises the power of faith coupled with prayer, indicating that faith is not a passive attribute but an active, living force that shapes our actions and outcomes.

THE NATURE OF FAITH

Understanding Faith as a Spiritual Force

Faith and God's Word are potent spiritual forces and weapons against the enemy.

The Apostle Paul, in **Ephesians 6:16**, speaks of faith as a shield,

"Above all, taking the shield of faith, wherewith ye shall be able to quench all the fiery darts of the wicked."

Faith, rooted in the promises of God's Word, serves as a defensive barrier, repelling the enemy's attacks, lies, and attempts to undermine our confidence in God.

Similarly, God's Word is portrayed as a sword in the same chapter, **Ephesians 6:17**,
"And take the helmet of salvation, and the sword of the Spirit, which is the word of God."

The Word of God is a divinely powerful weapon, cutting through deception and revealing truth. It's not just a collection of historical narratives or moral guidelines; it carries the power of the living God. By continually immersing ourselves in His Word, we sharpen this spiritual sword, ready to counteract the enemy's lies with God's truth and stand firm in our faith.

REFLECTION

1

A summary of what you learnt in this lesson:

1

How does this challenge you personally?

REFLECTION

REFLECTION

1

What is God saying to you personally?

REFLECTION

1

AT HOME: How will you apply this practically in your life? (your response to the last reflection question)

REFLECTION

1

GROUP DISCUSSION NOTES:

FOUNDATIONS OF FAITH

SESSION 2

Exploring Scriptural Instances of Faith

The Bible abounds with instances of faith, giving us examples of how trust in God can move mountains and bring forth miracles.

One remarkable instance is the story of the woman with an issue of blood in **Mark 5:25-34**. This woman, suffering for twelve years, believed that merely touching Jesus' cloak would heal her. And indeed, **her faith made her well**.

Her faith was active; it drove her to Jesus despite the crowd, and it made her whole.

Another poignant instance can be found in the Old Testament: the story of **Daniel in the lion's den (Daniel 6)**. Daniel was cast into a den of lions for praying to God, defying the king's decree. However, his unshakeable faith in God shut the mouths of the lions, and he emerged unscathed. Daniel's faith was not deterred by the immediate danger but remained firm, trusting in the protection of his God.

These instances highlight faith's power when we fully trust in God's promises and His ability to deliver us.

FOUNDATIONS OF FAITH

The Connection Between Faith and Works

The Bible clearly makes a vital connection between faith and works; faith is not merely an abstract belief but should be evidenced by our actions. **James 2:17** states,

"So also faith by itself, if it does not have works, is dead."

This verse highlights the truth that genuine faith results in actions that align with God's commandments and reflect His love. Our works, or actions, testify to the authenticity of our faith.

In the story of Rahab the harlot **(Joshua 2)**, her faith in the God of Israel was demonstrated in her works when she hid the Israelite spies and helped them escape. **Her actions were a clear manifestation of her belief in God's promise to Israel.**

Likewise, in the New Testament, the faith of the four men who brought a paralysed man to Jesus was evidenced by their work. They went to great lengths, even digging through a roof, to get their friend to Jesus **(Mark 2:1-12)**. **Jesus saw their faith through their actions** and as a result, the paralysed man was healed.

Therefore, our faith should always motivate our works, and through our works, our faith is made complete.

REFLECTION

2

A summary of what you learnt in this lesson:

REFLECTION

2

How does this challenge you personally?

REFLECTION

2

What is God saying to you personally?

REFLECTION

AT HOME: How will you apply this practically in your life? (your response to the last reflection question)

REFLECTION

2

GROUP DISCUSSION NOTES:

BUILDING A STRONG FAITH FOUNDATION:
Understanding Our Identity In Christ

SESSION 3

Who are We in Christ?

In Christ, we find not only our identity, but also our victory over sin and the devil.

Understanding who we are in Christ is the bedrock for a robust faith foundation and triumphant Christian life.
Romans 6:6 declares,
"We know that our old self was crucified with him in order that the body of sin might be brought to nothing, so that we would no longer be enslaved to sin."

Our identification with Christ in His death signifies the death of our sinful nature and thus our liberation from sin's power. The devil, who uses sin as a stronghold, is defeated in our lives because we are no longer under sin's power and control.

In addition to this, **1 John 4:4** affirms,
"Greater is He that is in you than he who is in the world."
This truth reminds us that the Spirit of Christ within us is more powerful than any demonic force against us. It is the indwelling Holy Spirit within that enables us to live victoriously over sin and the devil.

Therefore, comprehending our identity in Christ is crucial—it's not just about who we are, but Whose we are, and the divine power that backs us in our spiritual battles.

BUILDING A STRONG FAITH FOUNDATION:
Understanding Our Identity In Christ

The Role of Christ in Our Identity

The role of Christ in shaping our identity is pivotal and transformative.

When we come to faith in Jesus Christ, our identity becomes fundamentally and inseparably linked to Him. We are not only believers in Christ, but we become part of Christ—His body. As the Scripture says in **1 Corinthians 12:27**, *"Now you are the body of Christ and individually members of it."*

As members of His body, we are fortified with His strength, His righteousness, and His victorious life. We are not left to our own devices but are continually empowered and upheld by His grace. Christ's victory over sin, death, and the devil becomes our victory. In Him, we are more than conquerors. **Romans 8:37** declares, *"No, in all these things we are more than conquerors through him who loved us."*

Our identity in Christ not only alters who we are, but it also changes our position—we move from defeat to victory, from weakness to strength, and from fear to faith.
This victorious identity is what fortifies us in every trial and tribulation we face. Knowing that Christ is our source, our strength, and our victory empowers us to live a life that reflects His overcoming power.

REFLECTION

A summary of what you learnt in this lesson:

REFLECTION

3

How does this challenge you personally?

REFLECTION

3

What is God saying to you personally?

3

REFLECTION

AT HOME: How will you apply this practically in your life? (your response to the last reflection question)

REFLECTION

GROUP DISCUSSION NOTES:

SESSION 4

WALKING IN OUR IDENTITY IN CHRIST

Aligning Our Thoughts with Our Identity in Christ

Aligning our thoughts with our identity in Christ is a fundamental step towards living a victorious and faith-filled life.

As our identity is in Christ, so should our thoughts be. The Apostle Paul instructs us in 2 **Corinthians 10:5** to *"take captive every thought to make it obedient to Christ."*

This implies submitting our thoughts to the truth of God's Word and allowing that truth to re-shape our thinking. When doubts, fears, or feelings of unworthiness emerge, we must counteract them with the truth of our identity in Christ—we are God's beloved, chosen, and redeemed.

Similarly, **Romans 12:2 encourages us not to conform to the pattern of this world, but to be transformed by the renewing of our mind**. This transformation happens as we fill our minds with God's Word, aligning our thoughts with our identity in Christ.

As we continually renew our minds with the truth, we fortify our faith and walk in the victory that Christ has already won for us. This is not a passive process but an active commitment to think and believe in line with our true identity in Christ.

SESSION 4

WALKING IN OUR IDENTITY IN CHRIST

Practical ways to manifest our identity in Christ

Manifesting our identity in Christ involves living in a way that reflects our status as God's children and ambassadors of His kingdom.

It begins with daily communion with God through prayer and studying His Word. This constant communication fosters a deeper understanding of God's character and His promises, and deepens our love for Him, enabling us to live according to His will. As Jesus said in **John 15:5**,
"I am the vine; you are the branches. If you remain in me and I in you, you will bear much fruit; apart from me you can do nothing."

Living in Christ results in bearing the fruits of the Spirit as outlined in **Galatians 5:22-23**,
"But the fruit of the Spirit is love, joy, peace, forbearance, kindness, goodness, faithfulness, gentleness and self-control."
These fruits should be evident in our interactions with others, showing the world who we are in Christ.

Furthermore, we manifest our identity in Christ by standing firm in faith, regardless of the challenges we face.
Ephesians 6:13 encourages us,
"Therefore put on the full armour of God, so that when the day of evil comes, you may be able to stand your ground, and after you have done everything, to stand."
In standing firm, we reflect our identity as overcomers in Christ, fortified by faith and secure in the victory He has won for us.

WALKING IN OUR IDENTITY IN CHRIST

Using Scripture to affirm our identity

Scripture is a powerful tool for affirming our identity in Christ. It serves as a mirror reflecting who we are in Him and reinforces our faith in His promises.

For example, when we read in **1 Peter 2:9** that we are ***"a chosen people, a royal priesthood, a holy nation, God's special possession,"*** we should affirm this truth over our lives, believing and declaring that we are chosen, royal, and set apart for God's purposes.

Similarly, **Ephesians 1:7** reminds us that,
"In him we have redemption through his blood, the forgiveness of sins, in accordance with the riches of God's grace."

This scripture affirms our identity as redeemed and forgiven children of God. By regularly reading, meditating on, and speaking these scriptures aloud, we root our identity in the unchanging truth of God's Word rather than the changing circumstances of life.

Affirming our identity through scripture also builds resilience against the enemy's lies, equipping us to stand firm in faith and walk in the victory Christ has secured for us. Through scripture, we not only discover our identity in Christ, but we also embrace and internalise this truth, aided by the indwelling Spirit of God who guides us into all truth. As we receive divine revelation, it transforms our lives and influences our actions. This is not just 'positive thinking' Gods Word is supernatural and it literally brings transformation. As we do this it goes past head knowledge and gets into our spirit. Our life becomes one with the Word.

REFLECTION

A summary of what you learnt in this lesson:

4

How does this challenge you personally?

REFLECTION

REFLECTION

4

What is God saying to you personally?

4

AT HOME: How will you apply this practically in your life? (your response to the last reflection question)

REFLECTION

REFLECTION 4

GROUP DISCUSSION NOTES:

FREEDOM AND DELIVERANCE:
Understanding Deliverance

Biblical Understanding of Deliverance

Deliverance in the biblical context refers to the act of being set free from bondage or oppression, particularly of a spiritual nature.

It's a significant facet of salvation brought by Jesus Christ, who came to:
"proclaim freedom for the prisoners and recovery of sight for the blind, to set the oppressed free" **(Luke 4:18).**
In this scripture, Jesus announces His mission, which is fundamentally about liberation - liberation from sin, spiritual blindness, and all forms of oppression.

Another pivotal scripture that illustrates deliverance is **Colossians 1:13**, where Paul writes, *"He has delivered us from the domain of darkness and transferred us to the kingdom of his beloved Son."*

This deliverance is a transfer from the realm of darkness—representing sin, death, and the devil's authority—into the kingdom of Christ, which is characterised by light, life, and Jesus Christ's power and authority.

In essence, understanding deliverance from a biblical perspective involves recognising it as a transformative process, a change in spiritual authority, and a journey into freedom and abundant life in Christ. This freedom then forms a crucial part of our identity as disciples of Christ.

Deliverance often involves the casting out of demons, which is a practice firmly rooted in Scripture and demonstrated powerfully in the ministry of Jesus.

SESSION 5

In **Mark 1:34, we read,** *"And He [Jesus] healed many who were ill with various diseases, and cast out many demons; and He was not permitting the demons to speak, because they knew who He was."*

This verse not only underscores Jesus' authority over demonic forces but also reveals the link between physical ailments and demonic influence.

In **Luke 11:20, Jesus declares,** *"But if I drive out demons by the finger of God, then the kingdom of God has come upon you."*
Casting out demons is therefore a powerful manifestation of God's kingdom and power.

For believers today, the authority to cast out demons is not just restricted to Jesus or the apostles. **Mark 16:17** confirms this, stating:
"And these signs will accompany those who believe: In my name they will drive out demons..."

As followers of Christ, we are equipped with His authority to cast out demons, and through His name we can both experience deliverance and drive out demons in others, thereby enforcing the victory of Jesus over the forces of darkness.

FREEDOM AND DELIVERANCE:
Understanding Deliverance

How Deliverance Affects our Spiritual Journey

Deliverance is a transformative experience that significantly impacts our spiritual journey. It's like a rebirth into a new realm of spiritual freedom and enlightenment.

When we are delivered from demonic influences or bondages, we are essentially freed from spiritual hindrances that have been holding us back from fully experiencing God's love and grace.

In **Luke 8:2, Mary Magdalene, after being delivered from seven demons, became one of Jesus' most devoted followers.** Her deliverance transformed her spiritual journey, leading her to a profound encounter with the risen Christ.

Similarly, the story of the **Gerasene demoniac in Mark 5:1-20 provides a powerful illustration of this transformation.** This man, once tormented and isolated by a legion of demons, was delivered by Jesus. His deliverance led to a dramatic transformation: from a life of torment to peace, from isolation to proclamation. The man, now delivered, proclaimed what Jesus had done for him, impacting the lives of many others.

Such instances demonstrate how deliverance can ignite significant spiritual growth, open up new pathways for experiencing God's blessings, and empower us to share the message of deliverance and freedom with others.

REFLECTION

5

A summary of what you learnt in this lesson:

5 REFLECTION

How does this challenge you personally?

REFLECTION

5

What is God saying to you personally?

AT HOME: How will you apply this practically in your life? (your response to the last reflection question)

REFLECTION

REFLECTION

GROUP DISCUSSION NOTES:

MAINTAINING FREEDOM AFTER DELIVERANCE

Strategies to Stay Free from Demonic Influences

It must be understood that maintaining freedom after deliverance first starts with spiritual rebirth and the infilling of the Holy Spirit. Jesus taught in **John 3:3,** *"Truly, truly, I say to you, unless one is born again he cannot see the kingdom of God."*

Being born again marks the beginning of our new life in Christ, a life where we are not under the bondage of sin or demonic influences. It's this new birth that gives us a new identity, making us children of God and co-heirs with Christ.

However, being born again is just the starting point. Jesus also emphasised the necessity of being filled with the Holy Spirit.

In Acts 1:8, He declared, *"But you will receive power when the Holy Spirit has come upon you, and you will be my witnesses..."*
The Holy Spirit empowers us to live victoriously and resist demonic influences.

Jesus warns in **Matthew 12:43-45 that when a unclean spirit leaves a person, it wanders around and later decides to return to its previous home. If it finds the house unoccupied, it returns with seven other spirits more wicked than itself**. This underscores the vital need not just for deliverance, but for the person to be born again and filled with the Holy Spirit. An 'unoccupied' state suggests a life that, while perhaps cleaned up through deliverance, has not been filled with the presence, power, and influence of the Holy Spirit.

SESSION 6

Therefore, to maintain our deliverance and stay free from demonic influences, it is not enough to be merely delivered. We must be born again, filled with the Spirit, walking in step with Him, and continually welcoming His renewing and fortifying work in our lives. *(This is extremely important to understand, otherwise the person being delivered could end up in a worse state than before.)*

Obedience to God's commands is a cornerstone in maintaining deliverance and walking in continuous freedom. Obedience is not merely about following rules; it's about aligning our lives with God's Word and His divine order, which brings blessings and protection.

Obedience to God and shutting the door on sin, keeps the devil out. In **Deuteronomy 28:1-2**, the Bible outlines the blessings that come from obedience:

"If you fully obey the Lord your God and carefully follow all his commands... the Lord your God will set you high above all the nations on earth. All these blessings will come on you and accompany you if you obey the Lord your God."

Moreover, **1 John 5:18** provides a powerful promise for those who live in obedience:

"We know that anyone born of God does not continue to sin; the One who was born of God keeps them safe, and the evil one cannot harm them."

This scripture emphasises that when we are born of God and strive to live in obedience, the wicked one—the devil—cannot touch us. This is not because of our strength or righteousness, but rather it's because of the 'One' and His finished work on the cross.

Therefore, maintaining deliverance and walking in victory involves a commitment to obedience. As we live in obedience to God's Word, we step into the promise of divine protection where the wicked one cannot touch us. This promise serves as a fortress, protecting us and enabling us to live out our faith boldly and victoriously

MAINTAINING FREEDOM AFTER DELIVERANCE

The Role of Prayer, Faith, and Scripture in Maintaining Deliverance

Prayer, faith, and Scripture help form a foundation for maintaining deliverance and living in sustained freedom.

Prayer is a way we communicate with God, an avenue to express our gratitude, seek His guidance, and request His strength to remain free from any form of bondage. Jesus, in **Matthew 26:41**, underscored the importance of prayer in spiritual warfare, stating,
"Watch and pray so that you will not fall into temptation. The spirit is willing, but the flesh is weak."

A prayer-less life will leave us vulnerable and susceptible to the enemy's temptations.
Faith, on the other hand, which is our trust in God and His promises, in His power and goodness, not only secures our deliverance but also helps us maintain it.

Hebrews 11:6 declares, *"And without faith, it is impossible to please God, because anyone who comes to him must believe that he exists and that he rewards those who earnestly seek him."*

Faith is also described as a shield in **Ephesians chapter 6.**

SESSION 6

Finally, **Scripture serves as our spiritual nourishment and the sword of the Spirit (Ephesians 6:17).** It equips us with the truth to counteract the enemy's lies and provides us with God's promises to fortify our faith.

As Jesus exemplified in His temptation in the wilderness, effectively wielding Scripture can put the devil on the run **(Matthew 4:1-11)**.

Therefore, maintaining our deliverance requires:
- a consistent prayer life,
- unshakeable faith in God,
- and a deep, operational knowledge of Scripture.

These three pillars, working together, fortify our spiritual defences, enabling us to live in the freedom Christ has won for us.

REFLECTION

6

A summary of what you learnt in this lesson:

REFLECTION

6

How does this challenge you personally?

REFLECTION

6

What is God saying to you personally?

REFLECTION

6

AT HOME: How will you apply this practically in your life? (your response to the last reflection question)

_____
_____
_____
_____
_____
_____
_____
_____
_____
_____
_____
_____
_____
_____
_____
_____

REFLECTION

6

GROUP DISCUSSION NOTES:

GOD'S PROMISE OF HEALING:
Walking in Divine Health

Biblical Perspective on Divine Healing

Divine healing is a central theme in the Bible, underlining God's heart for His people's wellbeing and His power to heal and restore health. This promise of healing is woven into the Old and New Testaments.

In **Exodus 15:26**, God reveals Himself as Jehovah Rapha, meaning 'The Lord Who Heals', promising the Israelites, *"for I am the Lord, who heals you."* This name of God encapsulates His nature as our Healer.

In the New Testament, the healing ministry of Jesus demonstrates this aspect of God's nature. In **Acts 10:38**, we learn how
"God anointed Jesus of Nazareth with the Holy Spirit and power, and... he went around doing good and healing all who were under the power of the devil, because God was with him."

These healings were not random acts of kindness but a demonstration of the Kingdom of God and a fulfilment of **Isaiah 53:5**, which prophesied that *"by His wounds we are healed."*

Therefore, from a biblical perspective, divine healing is part of God's redemptive plan, an expression of His love and mercy, and a manifestation of His Kingdom. As believers, we can trust in God's promise of healing, knowing that just as He forgives all our sins,
He also heals all our diseases (Psalm 103:3). This assurance allows us to walk in divine health and maintain our deliverance, living in the fullness of the life Jesus came to give us.

GOD'S PROMISE OF HEALING: Walking In Divine Health

How to Claim God's Promise of Healing

Claiming God's promise of healing involves understanding His will, exercising our faith, and praying in alignment with His promises.

Firstly, we must understand that God's will for us is health and wholeness.
As **3 John 1:2 affirms,** *"Dear friend, I pray that you may enjoy good health and that all may go well with you, even as your soul is getting along well."*
God's desire is for us to prosper in all aspects of life, including our physical health. Once we understand this, we can then exercise our faith. Hebrews 11:1 defines faith as *"the assurance of things hoped for, the conviction of things not seen."*

When we have faith in God's healing promises, we believe that He can and desires to heal us, even before we see the physical manifestation of our healing. **We walk by faith, not by sight (2 Corinthians 5:7)**, and this applies to our health as well.

Finally, we must pray in accordance with God's will and promises. **James 5:15 declares,** *"And the prayer offered in faith will make the sick person well; the Lord will raise them up."*
When we pray, believing and declaring God's promises over our health, we activate our faith and open the door for God's healing power to operate in our lives.

Thus, claiming God's promise of healing involves a deep understanding of His will, unwavering faith in His ability, and prayers anchored in His promises. In this way, we can live in divine health and experience the fullness of life God intends for us.

REFLECTION

7

A summary of what you learnt in this lesson:

7

How does this challenge you personally?

REFLECTION

REFLECTION

7

What is God saying to you personally?

REFLECTION

7

AT HOME: How will you apply this practically in your life? (your response to the last reflection question)

REFLECTION 7

GROUP DISCUSSION NOTES:

MAINTAINING HEALING AND DIVINE HEALTH

Spiritual, Mental, and Physical Aspects of Maintaining Divine Health

Maintaining healing and divine health encompasses a) spiritual, b) mental, and c) physical dimensions.

a) Spiritually, we need to stay connected to God, our source of life and health. As **Proverbs 4:20-22** admonishes, *"My son, pay attention to what I say; turn your ear to my words... for they are life to those who find them and health to one's whole body."* Regularly engaging with God's Word and maintaining a vibrant prayer life is vital in fortifying our spiritual health.

b) Mentally, we must guard our thoughts, as they greatly impact our wellbeing.
Philippians 4:8 instructs, *"Finally, brothers and sisters, whatever is true, whatever is noble, whatever is right, whatever is pure, whatever is lovely, whatever is admirable—if anything is excellent or praiseworthy—think about such things."*
Adopting a positive, faith-filled mindset aligns our thoughts with God's promises and contributes to overall health.

c) Physically, we are called to honour our bodies as the temple of the Holy Spirit **(1 Corinthians 6:19-20)**. This implies being mindful of our physical habits, including diet, rest, and exercise. Good health practices can serve as practical ways to maintain healing and promote divine health.

SESSION 8

Thus, maintaining divine health involves balancing these three interconnected aspects: spiritual, mental, and physical.

By prioritising our relationship with God, cultivating a healthy mindset, and caring for our bodies, we can live in sustained health and wholeness.

In addition, an often overlooked but crucial element in maintaining divine health is the cultivation of joy.
The Bible says in **Proverbs 17:22, *"A cheerful heart is good medicine, but a crushed spirit dries up the bones."***

Joy, as a fruit of the Spirit (Galatians 5:22), carries a healing property and has a profound positive effect on our overall wellbeing. Cultivating a joyful heart, even in the face of challenges, helps to maintain our healing and can fortify our mental, physical, and spiritual health.

Thus, maintaining an attitude of joy, rooted in our faith and trust in God, is integral to walking in divine health.

MAINTAINING HEALING AND DIVINE HEALTH

Role of Faith, Obedience, and Wisdom in Sustaining Divine Health

Sustaining divine health requires the interplay of faith, obedience, and wisdom.

Faith, as discussed in **Hebrews 11:1**, is *"the assurance of things hoped for, the conviction of things not seen."*
In the context of divine health, faith involves trust in God's healing promises and confidence that He is continually working for our good, even when circumstances don't seem favourable.

Obedience plays a crucial role in maintaining divine health as it aligns our actions with God's instructions for living. **Deuteronomy 28:1-2** highlights the blessings, including health, that come with obedience to God's commandments. By obeying God's directives about living, whether spiritual principles or practical guidance on lifestyle and diet, we position ourselves in the pathway of His blessings.

Wisdom, on the other hand, enables us to make decisions that enhance our health. **Proverbs 3:7-8** advises, *"Do not be wise in your own eyes; fear the Lord and shun evil. This will bring health to your body and nourishment to your bones."* Divine wisdom helps us discern the right choices that lead to health and longevity.

Therefore, the intersection of faith, obedience, and wisdom creates a solid framework for sustaining divine health. Trusting in God's healing promises, aligning our lives with His commandments, and applying His wisdom in our daily decisions lead to a life marked by health, peace, and victory.

REFLECTION

A summary of what you learnt in this lesson:

REFLECTION

8 How does this challenge you personally?

REFLECTION

8

What is God saying to you personally?

AT HOME: How will you apply this practically in your life? (your response to the last reflection question)

REFLECTION

REFLECTION

GROUP DISCUSSION NOTES:

LIVING A VICTORIOUS LIFE:
Understanding Victory in Christ

The Reality of our Victory in Christ

Our victory in Christ is not just a theological concept or a future expectation; it's a present reality that shapes how we live our lives today.

In the crucifixion and resurrection of Jesus, we find the ultimate demonstration of victory over sin, death, and all forms of evil.
The apostle Paul writes in **1 Corinthians 15:57, *"But thanks be to God! He gives us the victory through our Lord Jesus Christ."***
This victory is not earned or achieved by our efforts; it is a gracious gift from God through Christ.

Moreover, in **Romans 8:37**, we read,
"No, in all these things we are more than conquerors through him who loved us."
As believers, we are not merely survivors; we are more than conquerors in Christ. This victory impacts every aspect of our lives. It influences our identity, our mindset, and our daily walk. It fortifies our faith, strengthens our resilience, and underpins our joy.

Therefore, understanding our victory in Christ means recognising that, because of Jesus, we are not fighting for victory; we are fighting from victory. Regardless of the battles we face, we can confidently affirm that in Christ, we are victorious.

This victorious life is not devoid of challenges, but it is characterised by peace and confidence, knowing that Christ has already won the ultimate victory for us.

LIVING A VICTORIOUS LIFE:
Understanding Victory in Christ

How to Walk in this Victory

Walking in the victory that Christ has won for us is an ongoing, daily commitment that requires faith, obedience, and active reliance on God's Word.

Faith is our first step - we must believe and embrace the truth that Jesus has already secured our victory. **Hebrews 11:1** states,
"Now faith is confidence in what we hope for and assurance about what we do not see."
This includes the unseen spiritual realities of our victory in Christ.

Obedience to God's Word and His commandments is an essential part of walking in victory. **1 John 2:3-5** assures us,
"We know that we have come to know him if we keep his commands. Whoever says, 'I know him,' but does not do what he commands is a liar, and the truth is not in that person. But if anyone obeys his word, love for God is truly made complete in them."

Obedience aligns us with God's will and helps us live out the victorious life Jesus has called us to.

Finally, actively using and declaring God's Word fortifies us in our victorious walk. **Ephesians 6:17** describes the Word of God as the **sword of the Spirit**. As we meditate on God's Word and use it to confront life's challenges, we affirm our victory and resist the enemy's attempts to **steal, kill, and destroy (John 10:10).**

Therefore, by persistently exercising our faith, obeying God's Word, and wielding the Scripture in every circumstance, we can effectively walk in the victory that is ours in Christ.

SESSION 9

Please note: in this work book I will repeat key scriptures and themes.

Repetition of key scriptures plays an integral role in grounding our faith and shaping our perspectives. This process aids in the transformation of our mind as instructed in Romans 12:2: "Do not conform to the pattern of this world, but be transformed by the renewing of your mind. Then you will be able to test and approve what God's will is—his good, pleasing and perfect will."

When we repeatedly meditate on and declare God's Word, these scriptures gradually replace negative thoughts, fears, and doubts with God's truth.

Moreover, repetition drives the scripture from our conscious mind into our subconscious, influencing our beliefs, attitudes, and actions. As a result, we not only know God's promises intellectually, but we also believe them from our hearts and apply them to our lives.

This practice of repeating scripture essentially fortifies our faith, equips us for spiritual battles, and enables us to live victoriously in Christ.

REFLECTION

9

A summary of what you learnt in this lesson:

9

REFLECTION

How does this challenge you personally?

REFLECTION

9

What is God saying to you personally?

REFLECTION 9

AT HOME: How will you apply this practically in your life? (your response to the last reflection question)

REFLECTION

GROUP DISCUSSION NOTES:

WALKING OUT A VICTORIOUS LIFE

Practical Steps to Live a Victorious Christian Life

Living a victorious Christian life involves practical, daily steps rooted in faith, obedience, and communion with God.

Firstly, it's essential to maintain a close, personal relationship with Jesus Christ, our source of victory.

Jesus said in John 15:5, *"I am the vine; you are the branches. If you remain in me and I in you, you will bear much fruit; apart from me you can do nothing."*

Staying connected to Jesus through prayer, worship, and Bible study is fundamental for our victorious living.

Next, regularly affirm and declare God's Word over your life. As discussed earlier, repetition of key scriptures reinforces God's truths in our hearts and minds.

Take **Ephesians 6:10 for example,** *"Finally, be strong in the Lord and in his mighty power."*

Regularly declaring such truths builds our faith and helps us walk in the victory Christ has won for us.

Living in obedience to God's commandments is another crucial step. As Jesus noted in **John 14:15,** *"If you love me, keep my commands."*
Our obedience reflects our love for God and positions us to experience His blessings, including the blessing of victorious living.

Lastly, keep a community of faith.

Hebrews 10:25 encourages us not to neglect meeting together as believers. The support, encouragement, and accountability we receive from our spiritual community can significantly help us in our journey to live victoriously.

Remember, the victorious Christian life is not a destination but a journey. It's a continual process of growing in our relationship with God, standing firm on His Word, obeying His commands, and fellowshipping with other believers.

As we faithfully take these practical steps, we can confidently walk out the victorious life that God has planned for us.

WALKING OUT A VICTORIOUS LIFE

Overcoming Obstacles and Challenges

As we strive to live a victorious Christian life, we will inevitably encounter obstacles and challenges. However, these difficulties do not negate our victory in Christ; instead, they present opportunities for us to exercise our faith and experience God's power in profound ways.

In James 1:2-4, we are encouraged to consider trials as pure joy because they produce perseverance, leading to maturity and completeness in our faith. Therefore, when we face difficulties, we should turn to God in prayer, standing firm on His promises and believing in His ability to deliver us.

Moreover, we can lean on the power of God's Word to overcome challenges. **Hebrews 4:12 describes the Word of God as living and active, sharper than any two-edged sword.** As we wield the sword of the Spirit, which is the Word of God **(Ephesians 6:17)**, we can dismantle lies, dispel fears, and conquer any obstacles that stand in our way.

Remember that we are not alone in our struggles. **God has given us the Holy Spirit to guide and empower us (John 14:26), and we have a community of believers for support and encouragement (Hebrews 10:24-25).**

As we depend on God, use His Word, and lean on our spiritual community, we can overcome any obstacle or challenge and continue to walk in the victory that is ours in Christ.

Lastly, consider the words of **Psalm 23:4**,
"Even though I walk through the valley of the shadow of death, I will fear no evil, for you are with me; your rod and your staff, they comfort me."

This scripture powerfully portrays our journey through challenging times. The 'valley of the shadow of death' metaphorically represents the darkest, most challenging situations we might encounter. Yet, we are assured that even in these seemingly hopeless situations, we need not fear. Why? Because our God, the Shepherd of our souls, is with us. His 'rod' representing His authority, and 'staff', His support, provide us with comfort and reassurance. They are our tools of victory in navigating any valley of shadow we may encounter.

Thus, no matter how challenging the obstacle, we can boldly echo the psalmist's confidence, knowing that we are not alone, and with God by our side, victory is assured.

As Christians, even if we were to face death in this life (of course we all have an appointed time), we never die! We simply get promoted to glory, to abide with God in eternity forever.

WALKING OUT A VICTORIOUS LIFE

Using Scripture to Maintain our Victory in Christ

Scripture is our powerful weapon and guide in maintaining our victory in Christ. It serves both as a defensive shield and an offensive sword in our spiritual battles, helping us withstand and overcome the enemy's attacks (Ephesians 6:16-17).

As we consistently read, meditate on, and apply the Word of God, we equip ourselves with divine truths that affirm our victory. Jesus Himself demonstrated this during His temptation in the wilderness. Each time Satan presented a temptation, **Jesus responded with, *"It is written,"* followed by a relevant scripture (Matthew 4:1-11).** This example underscores the power of the Word of God in maintaining our victory.

Romans 10:17 reminds us,
"So then faith comes by hearing, and hearing by the word of God."
The more we immerse ourselves in the Scriptures, the stronger our faith becomes, and the more effectively we can stand firm in our victory.

Furthermore, we should not only read and hear the Word but also speak it.
Proverbs 18:21 says, *"Death and life are in the power of the tongue."*
As we declare God's promises and truths over our lives, we reinforce our faith and position ourselves to experience and maintain our victory in Christ.

In conclusion, Scripture is a vital tool in maintaining our victory. As we continually engage with the Word—reading, meditating, applying, and declaring it—we can confidently uphold our victory in Christ, no matter the circumstances.

REFLECTION

10

A summary of what you learnt in this lesson:

REFLECTION

10

How does this challenge you personally?

REFLECTION

10

What is God saying to you personally?

AT HOME: How will you apply this practically in your life? (your response to the last reflection question)

REFLECTION

REFLECTION

10

GROUP DISCUSSION NOTES:

PERSONAL SPIRITUAL DEVELOPMENT
Developing a Personal Prayer Life

Importance of Personal Prayer

Personal prayer holds an indispensable place in our spiritual development and the maintenance of our victory in Christ.

As our direct line of communication with God, prayer is our opportunity to express our gratitude and worship, tell Him our heart's desires, seek God's will, and enjoy fellowship with our Heavenly Father.

In **Matthew 6:6**, Jesus emphasises the importance of personal prayer:
"But when you pray, go into your room, close the door and pray to your Father, who is unseen. Then your Father, who sees what is done in secret, will reward you."
This scripture highlights the personal, intimate nature of prayer. It's a private engagement between us and God, where we can be open, vulnerable, and honest.

The Apostle Paul, in **1 Thessalonians 5:17**, urges us to *"pray without ceasing."*
This admonition suggests that prayer should not just be an occasional practice, but a consistent, integral part of our lives. Through constant prayer, we keep our spirits attuned to God's voice, grow in our relationship with Him, and receive guidance and strength for our spiritual journey.

Personal prayer also plays a significant role in securing and maintaining our victory in Christ.
When we face challenges, we can bring our concerns to God in prayer, standing on His promises and declaring our victory **(Philippians 4:6-7).**

Therefore, developing a consistent personal prayer life is vital for our spiritual growth and victorious living.

Praying in tongues, also known as praying in the Spirit, holds significant importance in our spiritual lives.
Jude 1:20 tells us, *"But you, dear friends, by building yourselves up in your most holy faith and praying in the Holy Spirit, keep yourselves in God's love..."*

This form of prayer allows us to communicate with God beyond the confines of our human understanding, as we yield ourselves to the inspiration of the Holy Spirit.
When we pray in tongues, we essentially allow the Holy Spirit to intercede through us.

As **Romans 8:26** suggests, *"the Spirit helps us in our weakness. For we do not know what to pray for as we ought, but the Spirit himself intercedes for us with groanings too deep for words."*

Praying in tongues, therefore, enables us to pray according to God's perfect will, even when we are not certain of what or how to pray.

Moreover, praying in tongues strengthens and edifies us - it helps us to build ourselves up in faith.

As we engage in this spiritual practice, we bolster our faith, fortify our spiritual resilience, and position ourselves to walk in the fullness of our victory in Christ.

Indeed, the Apostle Paul provided valuable teaching on this subject to the Corinthian church.
In his first letter to them, **1 Corinthians 14:2, he said,** *"For anyone who speaks in a tongue does not speak to people but to God. Indeed, no one understands them; they utter mysteries by the Spirit."*

This emphasises the unique aspect of praying in tongues, underlining its supernatural, mysterious, and deeply personal nature. It also reiterates the truth that praying in tongues is a Spirit-led communication with God, strengthening our personal spiritual connection with Him.

PERSONAL SPIRITUAL DEVELOPMENT
Developing a Personal Prayer Life

Practical Tips for Improving your Prayer Life

Here are some practical tips that can help strengthen your relationship with God through prayer.

- **Set a Specific Time**: Make prayer a priority by scheduling it into your day just like any other important activity. Daniel, a prophet of God, set aside three specific times a day for prayer (Daniel 6:10).
- **Find a Quiet Space**: Jesus often withdrew to solitary places to pray (Luke 5:16). A quiet, private space can help eliminate distractions and cultivate a focused, intimate time with God.
- **Pray Scripture:** Incorporate Bible verses into your prayers. This not only aligns your prayers with God's Word but also enhances your understanding of scripture. Jesus, when tempted by the devil, responded with scriptures (Matthew 4:1-11).
- **Use the ACTS Model:** This stands for Adoration (glorifying God), Confession (repenting to God), Thanksgiving (expressing gratitude to God) and Supplication (Making requests to God). It's a simple guide to structure your prayers.
- **Keep a Prayer Journal**: Documenting your prayers can help keep track of your requests, God's answers, and how your relationship with Him evolves over time.

- **Pray in the Spirit**: As discussed earlier, praying in tongues, as guided by the Holy Spirit, can build your faith and strengthen your spiritual connection with God (Jude 1:20, 1 Corinthians 14:2).
- **Be Persistent**: Jesus taught about the importance of persistent prayer in Luke 18:1-8. Don't be discouraged if answers don't come immediately.
- **Listen:** Prayer is not a one-way communication. Spend time in silence during your prayer sessions to listen to what God might be saying to you.

Remember, the goal of prayer is to grow closer to God, express your faith, seek His will, and enjoy His presence. As you integrate these practices into your prayer life, expect a deeper, more enriching prayer experience.

And finally, **make prayer a lifestyl**e: The Apostle Paul's command in **1 Thessalonians 5:17** to *"pray without ceasing"* is not a call to non-stop verbal prayer, but to adopt a lifestyle of continual communion with God. This means living with a prayerful mindset, always being open to God's presence and guidance throughout the day. It's about keeping an ongoing spiritual dialogue with God, whether in your thoughts, spoken words, or even through your actions. This could include short prayers of gratitude when good things happen, quick prayers for wisdom during decision-making, or silent prayers for strength in a tough moment.

Making prayer a lifestyle fosters an ever-deepening relationship with God and a stronger awareness of His constant presence in your life

REFLECTION

11

A summary of what you learnt in this lesson:

REFLECTION 11

How does this challenge you personally?

REFLECTION

11

What is God saying to you personally?

REFLECTION 11

AT HOME: How will you apply this practically in your life? (your response to the last reflection question)

REFLECTION

11

GROUP DISCUSSION NOTES:

CONSISTENCY AND GROWTH IN FAITH

The Importance of Daily Devotions and Continuous Spiritual Growth

---

Consistency in our spiritual disciplines and a commitment to continuous growth in faith are crucial aspects of our Christian walk and discipleship .

Regular and meaningful engagement with God's Word, through daily devotions, nourishes our spiritual life much like food nourishes our physical bodies.
Psalm 119:105 declares,
"Your word is a lamp for my feet, a light on my path."
Engaging in daily devotions provides us with a greater awareness of Gods leading, illuminating our path and informing our decisions in alignment with God's will.

It also deepens our understanding of God, His character, and His promises, which fortifies our faith.

The Apostle Paul, in **2 Timothy 2:15**, encourages us to *"Study to shew thyself approved unto God, a workman that needeth not to be ashamed, rightly dividing the word of truth."*

This exhortation underlines the importance of diligent, consistent study of God's Word, which aids our growth in faith and maturity in Christ.

Furthermore, **Hebrews 6:1** urges us to *"go on unto perfection."*

This refers to our continuous spiritual growth. As believers, we're not meant to remain stagnant but are called to an ever-deepening relationship with God, going from glory to glory and strength to strength.

This progression requires a humble teachable heart, daily surrender, constant learning, and the practical application of God's Word to our lives.

Ultimately, daily devotions and continuous spiritual growth foster a thriving relationship with God, a solid faith foundation, and victory in our spiritual journey.
They allow us to draw nearer to God, grow in wisdom and understanding, and live out our faith more effectively.

CONSISTENCY AND GROWTH IN FAITH

Strategies for Remaining Consistent in Faith

Maintaining faith consistency is key to deepening our relationship with God and becoming steadfast in our Christian walk.
Here are some strategies to help cultivate this consistency:

- **Stay Rooted in God's Word**: Regular Bible study and meditation should be a cornerstone of your daily routine. Psalm 1:2-3 compares the blessed person who delights in God's law and meditates on it day and night to a tree planted by streams of water—healthy, fruitful, and unshakeable.
- **Prioritise Prayer:** Keep an ongoing dialogue with God through prayer. This vital spiritual discipline not only deepens your relationship with God but also builds your faith and dependency on Him.
- **Practice Fasting:** Fasting is a spiritual discipline that focuses your spirit and body on God. It helps you draw closer to God, become more sensitive to His leading, intensify your prayers and helps eliminate nagging doubts. (Acts 13:2-3).
- **Be Generous:** Practice giving tithes and offerings consistently, as well as showing generosity towards others. Jesus taught that it is more blessed to give than to receive (Acts 20:35). Giving not only expresses our trust in God's provision but also cultivates a heart of compassion and aligns us with God's generous nature.

SESSION 12

- **Engage in a Faith Community**: Join a local church or Bible study group. This provides a supportive environment that can encourage and strengthen your faith journey (Hebrews 10:24-25).
- **Apply Your Faith:** Live out your faith in your everyday life. Faith without action is dead. (James 2:26). Demonstrating your faith in tangible ways strengthens your faith and makes it more real to you and those around you.
- **Remember God's Faithfulness:** Reflect on God's past faithfulness and answered prayers. This serves as a constant reminder of His unchanging character and faithfulness (Psalm 77:11).
- **Cultivate Gratitude**: Make it a habit to express gratitude to God for all His blessings. This helps keep your focus on God's goodness and fosters a positive, faith-filled perspective.
- **Be filled with the Holy Spirit**: Seek to be continually filled with the Holy Spirit, who equips and empowers us to live out our faith (Ephesians 5:18).

By incorporating these practices into your life, you can strengthen your faith, become more rooted in God's Word, and enjoy a more dynamic and intimate relationship with Him.

REFLECTION

12

A summary of what you learnt in this lesson:

REFLECTION

12

How does this challenge you personally?

REFLECTION

12

What is God saying to you personally?

REFLECTION 12

AT HOME: How will you apply this practically in your life? (your response to the last reflection question)

REFLECTION

12

GROUP DISCUSSION NOTES:

FINAL REFLECTIONS

MOVING FORWARD IN YOUR FORTIFIED FAITH JOURNEY

As we bring our course to a close, I want to encourage you with this:

Step forth boldly and victoriously into your future.

Your faith, now fortified, serves as a powerful weapon and a shining beacon in this world. You are not merely called to exist, but to conquer.

You are not destined for the side lines, but for the forefront of a spiritual revival.

Your identity in Christ is not merely a title, but a truth - a declaration of victory over sin, over fear, and over every form of darkness. Let the reality of this victory echo in every aspect of your life - in your health, your actions, your thoughts, and your words.

Cherish your deliverance and fiercely protect it. You have been set free, and it's your mandate to live in that freedom, showing others the path to their own deliverance.

Stand firm in divine health, not as an abstract concept but as a lived reality. You are a testimony of God's healing power, an ambassador of His divine health here on earth.

With every step you take, walk in victory. Regardless of the challenges you face, remember the authority you have in Jesus. Each obstacle is an opportunity to experience and display the mighty power of God at work in your life.

FINAL REFLECTIONS

Believe for revival. Stir up faith within yourself and in those around you.

As you cultivate your prayer life, engage in fasting, and give generously.

May these spiritual disciplines not only draw you closer to God but also ignite a spark of revival that touches those around you.

As **Hebrews 11:1** tells us,
"Now faith is the assurance of things hoped for, the conviction of things not seen."
This assurance, this conviction, is what we carry - a vibrant, living faith that believes in the unseen and expects the miraculous.

You are not just finishing a course; you are beginning a renewed journey of faith, one of victory and revival.

God bless you as you march forward, your faith fortified, your spirit ignited, and your heart set on revival.

Amen!

DECLARATIONS

Finally I want to leave you with some powerful biblical declarations. Let me encourage you to get into the habit of declaring these truths everyday over your life and circumstances. Remember, life and death is in the power of the tongue.

As believers, the act of declaring God's Word over our lives is a potent practice of faith. This isn't about a positive confession or wishful thinking; it's about aligning our thoughts, words, and actions with the truth of God's Word.

Scripture affirms in Hebrews 4:12 that God's Word is living and active, sharper than any two-edged sword. It's not just a collection of old stories or nice sayings; it's God-breathed, infused with His life-changing power. When we speak His Word over our lives and circumstances, we are not merely reciting verses; we are proclaiming His promises, His character, His power, and His will.

In **Revelation 12:11**, we learn that we overcome the enemy ***"by the blood of the Lamb and by the word of our testimony."***

There is power in our spoken testimony, our declaration of what God has done and who He is.

When we declare God's Word, we stand against the lies and deceit of the enemy. We remind ourselves, and the spiritual realm, of our identity in Christ, our victory in Him, and the promises that we've been given.

The importance of declaring God's Word lies in its ability to shift our perspective, strengthen our faith, transform our minds, and align us more fully with God and His kingdom. So let's not underestimate the power of declaring His Word over our lives, **for our God watches over His Word to perform it (Jeremiah 1:12).**

Speak these declarations out loud over your life, believe them, and see how God's Word fortifies your faith and brings about transformation.

DECLARATIONS

- "I am more than a conqueror through Christ who strengthens me." (Romans 8:37)

- "God has not given me a spirit of fear, but of power, love, and a sound mind." (2 Timothy 1:7)

- "I am an overcomer by the blood of the Lamb and by the word of my testimony." (Revelation 12:11)

- "The same power that raised Christ from the dead is alive in me." (Ephesians 1:19-20)

- "I am God's workmanship, created in Christ Jesus for good works." (Ephesians 2:10)

- "No weapon formed against me shall prosper." (Isaiah 54:17)

- "I am healed by the stripes of Jesus." (1 Peter 2:24)

- "I have been delivered from the power of darkness and translated into the kingdom of God's dear Son." (Colossians 1:13)

- "The joy of the Lord is my strength." (Nehemiah 8:10)

- "I can do all things through Christ who strengthens me." (Philippians 4:13)

- "As I submit to God and resist the devil, he must flee from me." (James 4:7)

- "I am a new creation in Christ; old things have passed away; behold, all things have become new." (2 Corinthians 5:17)

DECLARATIONS

FINALLY

- "My body is the temple of the Holy Spirit, purchased at a price. I honour God with my body." (1 Corinthians 6:19-20)

- "I am not a slave to sin; I am free in Christ." (Romans 6:6)

- "I am complete in Him who is the head of all principality and power." (Colossians 2:10)

- "I am an ambassador for Christ, bringing reconciliation to the world."
(2 Corinthians 5:20)

- "The Lord is my shepherd; I lack nothing. He leads me in paths of righteousness for His name's sake." (Psalm 23:1,3)

- "I have the mind of Christ, and I hold the thoughts, feelings, and purposes of His heart." (1 Corinthians 2:16)

- "As I abide in Him, and His words abide in me, I will ask what I desire, and it shall be done for me." (John 15:7)

- "I am victorious in Christ. For God always causes me to triumph in Christ." (2 Corinthians 2:14)

www.ingramcontent.com/pod-product-compliance
Lightning Source LLC
Chambersburg PA
CBHW061138010526
44107CB00069B/2979